100 Math Workouts
and Practical Teaching Tips

An Essential Tool for Today's Middle School Mathematics Teachers

Based on Middle School Math Standards and Curricula

Written by Tony G. Williams, Ed.D.

Illustrated by Corbin Hillam

Teaching & Learning Company
1204 Buchanan St., P.O. Box 10
Carthage, IL 62321-0010

This book belongs to

_____

Dedications

Dedicated to my parents,
Jean and Grady,
who are retired math teachers;
and to my wife, Sharon;
and our triplets—TLC
(Tony, Leah and Christina).

Cover design by Sara King.

Copyright © 2008, Teaching & Learning Company

ISBN 13: 978-1-57310-543-9

ISBN 10: 1-57310-543-0

Printing No. 987654321

Teaching & Learning Company
1204 Buchanan St., P.O. Box 10
Carthage, IL 62321-0010

At the time of publication, every effort was made to insure the accuracy of the information included in this book. However, we cannot guarantee that the agencies and organizations mentioned will continue to operate or to maintain these current locations.

Dear Teacher or Parent,

In this book, you will find a comprehensive collection of mathematics-related work-out activities and practical teaching tips for today's middle school math teachers. In an age where teachers must compete for their students' attention against a number of influences (television, video games, Internet, peer pressure and other social factors), it is even more critical to develop lessons that capture students' interest, that promote and enhance the desire for learning, and that reinforce fundamental math skills. This resource book includes 100 sensational math workouts designed especially to engage students' exploration of mathematics by providing fun thought-provoking, interesting, skill-building, math-related activities. Students will see that math can be fun and exciting.

The workout process is a vital part of any lesson. It should be an inviting, settling and stimulating process that readies students for that day's lesson. The best way to start a math lesson is with a workout that engages students with mathematics. This resource book can help turn on the "light" within students and foster curiosity for mathematics. Not only are these workouts fun, they are based on middle school math standards and curricula. Each workout is presented on a ready-to-use, reproducibles. Each workout also includes a solution key or mini-lesson with background, discussion, strategy and demonstration for solving each problem. These workouts can be easily copied as transparencies for full-class instruction and discussion.

At the end of the book are 10 practical teaching tips for today's classroom. These practical techniques and strategies address specifically the current demands and challenges facing today's teachers, particularly in large urban school settings. The tips cover a broad spectrum of critical areas, ranging from class-room management to the use of technology to parental involvement. This resource book also includes suggestions for the use of the workouts and a bi-weekly workout sheet that can be used to track the workout work.

I hope you find these workouts useful as you introduce your students to the exciting world of mathematics.

Sincerely,

Tony

Tony G. Williams, Ed.D.

TABLE OF CONTENTS

Unit 1
Mathematics Exploration and Curiosity

Unit 2
Critical Thinking and Logic

Unit 3
Sports, Games and Other Fun

TLC10543 Copyright © Teaching & Learning Company, Carthage, IL 62321

Unit 4
Math Concepts, Analysis and Computation

Unit 5
Application, Pre-Algebra and Mastery

ACTIVITY SUGGESTIONS

Introduction

In this resource book, you will find 100 math workouts that support your math curricula. Each workout was designed as a student activity and class discussion for the first two to seven minutes of class. The workouts cover a broad range of mathematics exploration, from critical thinking to pure fun. The workouts are presented in five units:

1. Mathematics Exploration and Curiosity
2. Critical Thinking and Logic
3. Sports, Games and Other Fun
4. Math Concepts, Analysis and Computation
5. Application, Pre-Algebra and Mastery

Teachers know that workouts are an effective tool in teaching mathematics. Workouts also allow teachers a few valuable minutes for administrative duties (attendance, announcements, etc.) while settling students for the upcoming lesson. Here are some suggestions to help you get the most out of the workouts in this book.

The Daily Workouts Sheet and Sequence

The workouts in this book should be used with the Daily Workouts Sheet on page 8 (or a similar form developed by the teacher). Each Daily Workouts Sheet (front and back) can be used for 20 workouts or approximately four weeks of activities.

The workout activities can be used with related or unrelated lesson materials. While they are organized by category, you are encouraged to skip around and use the activity that best suits the need for the day. Note: There are a few workouts where a prerequisite skill is involved (e.g. finding the additive inverse and subtraction integers).

Using the Workouts

Each day's workout should be projected on the ove head screen as students enter the classroom. Onc seated, students should immediately begin the activit You can read or assign a student to read the activity t assist students whose view is obstructed or who ar visually impaired. If it is a more complex workout, yc should also explain the activity in more detail. The wor out activities are designed to last from two to seven mi utes. During this time, walk around the classroom t make sure all students are on task and understand th activity. You can also use this time to take attendanc check homework, return/collect papers, mal announcements or do other administrative tasks.

At the end of the workout, initiate a discussion abo the solution. Ask for volunteers or call on students f responses. Allow one to two additional minutes f related discussion and questions. You could also use overhead transparency of the solution key to genera discussion.

Grading Workouts

It is important that the workouts are incorporated into students' grade so students recognize their value. It is recommended that the workouts be worth 5%-10% of each student's grade. The workout sheets should be collected and evaluated by the teacher on a periodic basis. Workouts should be graded primarily on the effort of students. Because the workouts serve to reinforce skills, introduce new ideas and explore the fun applications of mathematics, the effort should outweigh correctness of response.

Workout for Success

The workout process is a vital part of any lesson. It should be an inviting, stimulating process that readies students for that day's lesson. There is no better way to start a math lesson than with a workout that excites students about math.

Workout Responses

Workout activities are divided into three types: 1. computational; 2. choice (multiple choice, true or false, or educated guess) and 3. explanatory. For computational workouts, encourage students to show as much work as possible on the workout sheet. Evaluate this type of workout based on work shown by the student.

Some workouts will give students a choice (multiple choice or true/false) for the response. Encourage students to express on their answer sheets (and orally during the discussion) their reasoning for making a particular choice. In evaluating these workout responses, look for clarity of expression as well as logic and creativity.

Finally, there are workouts that require students to draw conclusions and explain their results in writing. In addition to math skills, good writing and reading skills are essential for students' success. These workouts will provide an excellent opportunity for teachers to further develop students' reading, writing and communication skills. Encourage students to express the reasoning or logic behind their decisions. For these types of workouts, evaluate students according to the quality of their written explanation.

Daily Workouts

Student: _____ Teacher: _____ Period: _____

Week of _____ – _____   Week of _____ – _____

Score/Grade _____   Score/Grade _____

Monday _____ Activity: _____ Answer:	Monday _____ Activity: _____ Answer:
Tuesday _____ Activity: _____ Answer:	Tuesday _____ Activity: _____ Answer:
Wednesday _____ Activity: _____ Answer:	Wednesday _____ Activity: _____ Answer:
Thursday _____ Activity: _____ Answer:	Thursday _____ Activity: _____ Answer:
Friday _____ Activity: _____ Answer:	Friday _____ Activity: _____ Answer:

TLC10543 Copyright © Teaching & Learning Company, Carthage, IL 62321-0

A Calculated Greeting

On your calculator solve this problem:

$$.0014 + 6.71 - 6.5 + .562 = \underline{\qquad}$$

Then turn your calculator upside down for a special greeting.

What a Coincidence!

Follow these directions:

Choose any number between one and ten. _____
Multiply your number by nine. Then add the digits together. _____
Subtract three. _____
Find the letter of the alphabet that corresponds with your current number (1 = A, 2 = B, etc.).
_____
Select a state in the U.S. that starts with the same letter of the alphabet. _____
Then take the second letter in the spelling of the state and select a circus animal that starts with that letter. _____
What state and circus animal did you choose? _____

Solution #1

hELLO

.0014 + 6.71 – 6.5 + .562

= 0.7734

Upside down it resembles
hELLO.

This trick works for any problem with a solution of 0.7734.
Can you write another equation that gives this answer?

Solution #2

Lion in Florida

Did you choose the state of Florida and a lion? Chances are you did and so did most of your classmates. What a coincidence!

Explanation
It did not matter which number you chose in step one. When you multiply a number by nine, the digits always add up to nine. So when you subtract three, the result will always be six.

The sixth letter of the alphabet is "F," and Florida is the only state that starts with that letter. The second letter in *Florida* is "L," and the lion is the most popular circus animal that starts with that letter. How many people in your class chose the leopard?

Help Wanted

Because you are an excellent math student, you are taking a summer job as a math tutor. Which of the two jobs would let you make the most money?

Classifieds

a. TUTOR WANTED: Mrs. Richman is looking for a tutor for her son, Grady. Mrs. Richman will pay $10,000 for 30 days of work.

b. TUTOR WANTED: Mr. Miser wants a tutor for his daughter, Lucy. The pay is 1 cent per day for 30 days. But if you do a good job, Mr. Miser will double your salary each day (For example: Day 1 = 1 cent, Day 2 = 2 cents, etc.).

For the Curious

You know about thousands, millions, billions and even trillions. However, can you read the following numbers?

1,000,000,000,000,000

1,000,000,000,000,000,000

1,000,000,000,000,000,000,000

1,000,000,000,000,000,000,000,000

Solution #3

Hopefully, you chose job "b" with Mr. Miser and his daughter, Lu...
At one cent a day doubled for 30 days, you would earn more th...
$10,000,000. Let's see how that is possible:

Day	Exponent	Daily Pay	Total Pay	Day	Exponent	Daily Pay	Total Pay	Day	Exponent	Daily Pay	Total P...
1	2^0	$.01	$.01	11	2^{10}	$10.24	$20.47	21	2^{20}	$10,485.76	$20,971.
2	2^1	.02	.03	12	2^{11}	20.48	40.95	22	2^{21}	20,971.52	41,943.
3	2^2	.04	.07	13	2^{12}	40.96	81.91	23	2^{22}	41,943.04	83,886.
4	2^3	.08	.15	14	2^{13}	81.92	163.83	24	2^{23}	83,886.08	167,772.
5	2^4	.16	.31	15	2^{14}	163.84	327.67	25	2^{24}	167,772.16	335,544.
6	2^5	.32	.63	16	2^{15}	327.68	655.35	26	2^{25}	335,544.32	671,088.
7	2^6	.64	1.27	17	2^{16}	655.36	1,310.71	27	2^{26}	671,088.64	1,342,200
8	2^7	1.28	2.55	18	2^{17}	1,310.72	2,621.43	28	2^{27}	1,342,200.00	2,684,400
9	2^8	2.56	5.11	19	2^{18}	2,621.44	5,242.87	29	2^{28}	2,684,400.00	5,368,800
10	2^9	5.12	10.23	20	2^{19}	5,242.88	10,485.75	30	2^{29}	5,368,800.00	10,737,500

Solution #4

The answers are as follows:

A quadrillion is a one followed by 15 zeros (1,000,000,000,000,000).

A quintillion is a one followed by 18 zeros (1,000,000,000,000,000,000).

A sextillion is one followed by 21 zeros (1,000,000,000,000,000,000,000).

A septillion is one followed by 24 zeros (1,000,000,000,000,000,000,000,000).

How many zeros are there in one million, one billion and one trillion?

Up, Up and Away

The Robinson Family (Mr. Robinson, Mrs. Robinson, their son Jack and daughter Jillian) live across a canyon. The only way to their home is by hot air balloon. There must always be someone in the balloon to control it. The balloon cannot carry more than 200 pounds on each trip.

Mr. Robinson weighs 150 pounds, Mrs. Robinson weighs 125 pounds, Jack and Jillian each weigh 100 pounds. Can you get the Robinson family across the canyon to their home? How many trips does it take?

Unit 1 Mathematics Exploration and Curiosity

Mathematico, The Magician

Ms. Doubtfire took three of her students—Bob, Jake and Keisha—to see Mathematico, the famous magician. Each student paid $10 for a total of $30, to see Mathematico. Because Mathematico a friend of Ms. Doubtfire, he gave her back 5 one-dollar bills to share with the students. Ms. Doubtfire gave each student one dollar back and kept two dollars for gas and parking.

During his performance, Mathematico asked Bob, Jake and Keisha to come on stage. "How much did it cost each of you to attend this performance?" Mathematico asked. After careful thought, the students responded, "$9." "But how could that be?" Mathematico shouted. "3 times 9 equals, plus the $2 Ms. Doubtfire kept for gas and parking makes only $29. You are missing a dollar."

Where is the missing dollar?

Solution #5

The answer is:

1. Jack and Jillian take the balloon home.
2. One kid stays and the other returns with the balloon.
3. One of the parents takes the balloon home.
4. The parent stays home while the kid takes the balloon across the canyon.
5. Next, both kids take the balloon home.
6. One kid stays and the other goes back across the canyon.
7. Then the second parent takes the balloon home.
8. The second parent stays home while the kid takes the balloon across the canyon.
9. Finally, both kids take the balloon home.

Solution #6

There is no missing dollar!

Actually, the students only paid $25 dollars to see the show because 5 were returned by Mathematico. They each contributed to the $2 for parking and gas. The price of the each ticket was $8.33 ($8\frac{1}{3}$).

Solution:

$8\frac{1}{3} \times 3 = \$25$

$\$25 + \$2 \text{ (gas and parking)} = \$27$

$\$27 + \$3 \text{ (\$ back from Mathematico)} = \$30$

Workout #7

A Neat Calculator Trick

Choose any three-digit number and enter it in your calculator. Enter the same three digits again (For example: 123 becomes 123123). Use your calculator to divide the number by 13. Then divide the answer by 11. Finally, divide that number by 7. What is your result?

Careers in Mathematics

Workout #8

Math skills are important for everyone.

Directions: List 10 careers that depend heavily on good math skills and a knowledge of mathematics.

Solution #7

The result is your original three-digit number.

Why does this work?

Explanation

13 x 11 x 7 = 1001. When you multiply any three-digit number by 1001, the digits repeat themselves. For example, 123 x

---

Solution #8

Here are just a few of the possible careers.

What did you have that's not on this list?

Accountant	Economist	Principal
Administrator	Filmmaker	Professor
Architect	Lawyer	Programmer
Astronaut	Manager	Researcher
Banker	Mathematician	Salesperson
Chef	Mechanic	Scientist
Chemist	Meteorologist	Statistician
Choreographer	Nurse	Teacher
Director	Physicist	Technician
Doctor	Politician	

*As you can see, math is important to all of us.

Factorials!

Workout #9

What are factorials?

A **factorial** is the product of all numbers equal to and less than a number. The symbol for a factorial is "!"

For example: 4! = 4 x 3 x 2 x 1 = 24

Practice by computing the following:

3! =

5! =

4! - 2! =

Find Your Birthday

Workout #10

1. Take the number for the month you were born (Jan. = 1, Feb. = 2, etc.) _____
2. Multiply by 4. _____
3. Add 13. _____
4. Multiply by 25. _____
5. Subtract 200. _____
6. Add the day of the month you were born. _____
7. Multiply by 2. _____
8. Subtract 40. _____
9. Multiply by 50. _____
10. Add the last 2 digits of the year you were born (i.e. if born in 1971 add 71). _____
11. Subtract 10,500. _____
12. Now, what do you have? _____

The answers are:

3! = 3 x 2 x 1 = 6
3! = 6 (3 x 2 x 1)

5! = 5 x 4 x 3 x 2 x 1 = 120
5! = 120 (5 x 4 x 3 x 2 x 1)

4! - 2! = (4 x 3 x 2 x 1) – (2 x 1) = 24 – 2 = 22
4! – 2! = 22 (4 x 3 x 2 x 1) – (2 x 1)

Note: Factorials are often used in calculations involving statistics and probability.

Solution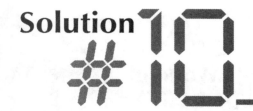

The answer is your birthday.

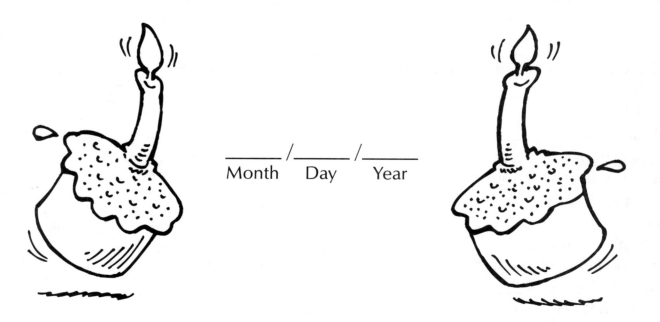

_____/_____/_____
Month   Day   Year

Let's Rock

Choose any number from 11 – 19. _____

Add the digits together. Then subtract the sum from your original number. _____

Multiply the new number by 9. _____

Add those digits together. _____

Subtract two. Then find the letter of the alphabet that corresponds to that number
(1 = A, 2 = B, etc.). _____

Think of a color that begins with that letter. _____

Then think of a musical instrument that begins with the same letter. _____

What did you think of? _____

It's Only a Trillion!

saying one number every second, how
ng would it take you to count to one trillion?

32 hours
32 days
32 years
32,000 years

2,522,880,000

The answer is:

Let's rock with a Green Guitar!

d. 32,000 years

It would take you approximately 32,000 years.

Here's how:
- 60 numbers per 1 minute
- 3600 numbers per 1 hour (60 x 60)
- 86,400 numbers per day (3,600 x 24)
- 31,536,000 numbers per year (86,400 x 365)
- Therefore 1,000,000,000,000 ÷ 31,536,000 = 31,700 years

UNIT 1 Mathematics Exploration and Curiosity

Mathematicians

Workout #13

Directions: Test your knowledge of famous mathematicians by matching them to their accomplishments.

a. Euclid (330-275 BC)
b. Sir Isaac Newton (1642-1727)
c. Blaise Pascal (1623-1662)
d. Pythagoras (580-500 BC)

_____ 1.   Invented calculus and contributed to our understanding of motion, gravity and light.

_____ 2.   Developed a theorem on the right triangle expressing $a^2 + b^2 = c^2$.

_____ 3.   Greek mathematician who founded geometry.

_____ 4.   French mathematician who invented the first calculating device.

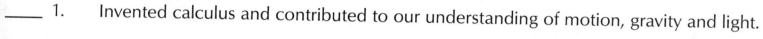

UNIT 1 Mathematics Exploration and Curiosity

Polygon Perfection

Workout #14

A polygon is a closed geometric figure whose sides are segments. They are named based on the number of sides.

Name the following polygons:

Polygon Name	Number of Sides
	3
	4
	5
	6
	7
	8
	9
	10
	12

Sir Isaac Newton: Invented calculus and contributed to the understanding of motion, gravity and light.

Pythagoras: Developed a theorem on the right triangle, expressing $a^2 + b^2 = c^2$.

Euclid: Greek mathematician who founded geometry.

Blaise Pascal: French mathematician who invented the first calculating device.

Solution

The answers are:

Polygon Name	Number of Sides
triangle	3
quadrilateral	4
pentagon	5
hexagon	6
heptagon	7
octagon	8
nonagon	9
decagon	10
dodecagon	12

frican-American Mathematicians

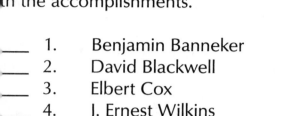

rican-Americans have made great contributions to mathe-
atics. A few of the great African-American mathematicians
e listed below. Test your knowledge by matching the names
th the accomplishments.

___ 1. Benjamin Banneker
___ 2. David Blackwell
___ 3. Elbert Cox
___ 4. J. Ernest Wilkins

First African-American to earn a Ph.D. in mathematics
Recognized as the first African-American mathematician;
taught himself calculus and trigonometry
Former president of the American Nuclear Society
First African-American named to the National Academy of Sciences

---

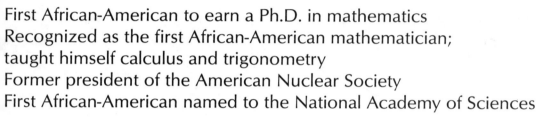

True or False?

ALRIGHT!

If $2^3 = 8$,
does $2^{-3} = -8$?

Solution #15

1. b.; 2. d.; 3. a.; 4. c.

Elbert Cox: First African-American to earn a Ph.D. in mathematics

Benjamin Banneker: Recognized as the first African-American mathematician; taught himself calculus and trigonometry

J. Ernest Wilkins: Former president of the American Nuclear Society

David Blackwell: First African-American named to the National Academy of Sciences

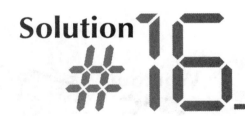

Solution #16

The correct answer is false.

Why?

A negative exponent is more representative of a fraction than a negative number.

So:

$$x^{-a} = 1/x^a$$

For example:

$$2^{-3} = 1/2^3 = 1/8$$

Other examples:

$$2^{-1} = 1/2$$

$$4^{-2} = 1/16$$

$$3^{-3} = 1/27$$

$$5^{-2} = 1/25$$

Life's Minutes

How many minutes have you been alive?

(Assume one year has 365 days.
We will ignore leap years for this problem.)

UNIT 2 Critical Thinking and Logic

Four Friends

When four friends get together, each friend
shakes hands with all the other friends.
How many total handshakes will there be?

Solution #17

To get the correct answer you:

1. Take your age in years and multiply by 365.
2. Add how many days it has been since your last birthday.
3. Then multiply by 24. Multiply that answer by 60.

Here are the approximate answers for the following ages:

12-year-old = 6,307,200 minutes
13-year-old = 6,832,800 minutes
14-year-old = 7,358,400 minutes

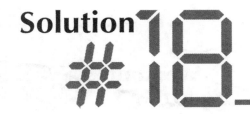

Solution #18

6 handshakes

Remember that a handshake is mutual. When you shake hands with someone, that person is also shaking hands with you. If the four friends' names were A, B, C and D, the following handshakes would occur:

1. A and B
2. A and C
3. A and D
4. B and C
5. B and D
6. C and D

Test Your Logical Reasoning

Workout #19

Alex, Laura, Jamal and Missy each participate in a different sport. Their sports are track, golf, tennis and basketball. Laura is the sister of the tennis player. Missy's sport does not use a ball. Jamal once made a birdie in his sport. Which sport does each play?

Is There a Connection?

Workout #20

a. 18 is to 81 as 86 is to what? Think about it! _____

Hint: The answer is not 68.

b. Fill in the correct operations (+ or – only) to make the equation true.

$$3 \_ 4 \_ 2 \_ 6 \_ 5 = 6$$

Solution #19

Jamal is the golfer, Missy runs track,
Laura plays basketball and Alex plays tennis.

Hint: One of the best strategies in solving logical reasoning problems is to make a table. Fill in the facts as you receive them:

	Alex	Laura	Jamal	Missy
Track	no	no	no	yes
Tennis	yes	no	no	no
Basketball	no	yes	no	no
Golf	no	no	yes	no

Solution #20

The answers are:

a. 98
Turn the first number upside down.

b. 3 + 4 – 2 + 6 – 5 = 6

Spending Change

Workout #21

Anita has $2.40 in change. If she has the same number of quarters, dimes and nickels, how many of each does she have?

UNIT 2 Critical Thinking and Logic

Logical Sequences

Workout #22

Directions: Find the number that will logically continue each of the sequences:

a.   1, 1, 2, 3, 5, 8, 13, ___

b.   11, 13, 17, 25, 32, 37, ___

Solution #21

6

$$
\begin{array}{lll}
6 \text{ quarters} = 6 \times .25 = & 1.50 \\
6 \text{ dimes} = 6 \times .10 = & .60 \\
6 \text{ nickels} = 6 \times .05 = & \underline{.30} \\
& \$2.40
\end{array}
$$

Solution #22

a. 21   b. 47

a. 1, 1, 2, 3, 5, 8, 13, 21

Pattern: Add the number that precedes the given number.
For example, 2 + 1= 3; 3 + 2 = 5; 5 + 3 = 8; 8 + 5 = 13; etc.

b. 11, 13, 17, 25, 32, 37, 47

Pattern: Add the digits of the given number to get the next number.
For example, 11 + (1 + 1) = 13; 13 + (1 + 3) = 17; 17 + (1 + 7) = 25;
25 + (2 + 5) = 32; etc.

Brainteasers

1. If you read pages 7-20, how pages have you read? _____

2. Why is 6 afraid of 7? _____

3. Cindy is taller than Karen. Karen is taller than Marcy. Marcy is taller than Quiana. Who is the tallest? _____

4. If you can dig a hole 30 minutes, how long will it take to dig half a hole? _____

5. How many hours is it from 12:00 p.m. on Saturday to 12:00 a.m. on Sunday? _____

- -

Fun at the Circus

Zorgo, Curly and Frizzie are members of the circus. They are a clown, a ringmaster and an elephant trainer, although not necessarily in that order.

1. Curly has curly hair.
2. Frizzie has red hair.
3. The elephant trainer is taller than Frizzie.
4. The clown is bald.

Who is the clown, the ringmaster and the elephant trainer?

Solution #23

The answers are:

1. 14

2. Because 7 ate (eight) 9.

3. Cindy

4. There is no such thing as a half a hole.

5. 12 hours

Solution #24

Curly is the elephant trainer, Frizzie is the ringmaster a Zorgo is the clown.

Did you make a table that looked like this?

	Clown	Elephant Trainer	Ringmaster
Curly	no	yes	no
Frizzie	no	no	yes
Zorgo	yes	no	no

Short and Fun!

. What's next in this sequence?

0, 1, 1, 2, 3, 5, 8, ____

. Which would you prefer, a full box of nickels or a half box of dimes?

Why? _____

Juan caught more fish than Maria but fewer than Sam.

Who caught the most fish? _____

Who caught the fewest? _____

Going to School

Terrence, Sarah and Lamont arrived at school on
roller blades, a moped and a bicycle.
The rider of the bicycle was a boy.
On his way to school, Terrence had to stop for gas.
How did each person get to school?

The answers are:

a. 13—Add the number that precedes the given number.

b. If you want the most money, you should pick the half box of dimes. Dimes are smaller and take less room; therefore, more dimes will fit.

c. Sam caught the most fish. Maria caught the fewest fish.

Solution **#26**

Sarah used roller blades, Terrence rode a moped and Lam rode a bicycle.

Did you make a table like the one below?

	Terrence	Sarah	Lamont
roller blades	no	yes	no
moped	yes	no	no
bicycle	no	no	yes

Penny for Your Thoughts

Workout #27

In a group of seven pennies, one penny weighs slightly less than the others. If you use a balance scale, what is the fewest number of times you will need to measure to determine which penny weighs less?

Who Did It?

Workout #28

It has been established that only 1 of 4 people committed a crime. The following statements were made by each suspect:

Jill: "Will did it."
Will: "Phil did it."
Bill: "I didn't do it."
Phil: "Will lied when he said I did it."

If only one statement is true, who did it?

Solution

One measurement is possible; however, the minimum numb of measurements is more commonly two.

Explanation

1 measurement: The best method to solve this problem is to place three pennies on one side of the scale and three pennies on the other side, leaving one penny out. If both sides weigh the same, then the remaining penny is the lightest one.

2 measurements: If one side is lighter than the other, then the lightest penny is in that group. Take two of the three pennies in the lightest group and place one on each side of the scale. If one of the pennies is lighter than the other, then that is the lightest penny. If the two pennies weigh the same, then the lightest penny is the third one from that group.

Solution

Bill did it.

Explanation

Will's statement "Phil did it" is the opposite of Phil's statement "Will lied when he said I did it"; therefore, one of those statements has to be the true statement. If Will's statement is true, that means Bill's statement "I didn't do it" is false. We then have two suspects: Bill and Phil.

Therefore, Phil's statement has to be the true, making all the other statements false. This means that Bill's statement "I didn't do it" is false. He is the one who committed the crime.

Workout
#29

What's Next?

a. Find a word that would logically come next in this list:

cat, dog, elephant, frog, _____

b. What is the next letter in this list:

O T T F F S S E ____

UNIT 2 Critical Thinking and Logic

Workout
#30

The Great Rectangular Divide

By drawing four straight lines, what is the greatest number of sections this rectangle can be divided into?

The answers are:

a. an animal that starts with "g" (gorilla, giraffe, etc.)

b. N (nine—the first letters of numbers 1-9)

**Solution**

11 sections

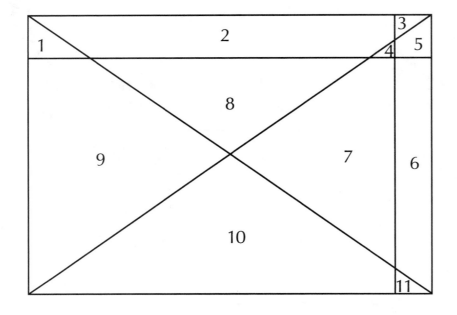

More Brainteasers

A boy and a girl are born on the same day of the same year to the same parents, but are not twins. How is this possible? _____

Which number does not fit the pattern of the other numbers?

2, 3, 6, 7, 8, 14, 15, 30

UNIT 3 **Sports, Games and Other Fun**

Test Your Telephone Memory

Hello?

Without looking at a phone, what are the numbers used to dial 1-800-FOR-MATH?

Is this 1-800-FOR-MATH?

The answers are:

a. They are part of a set of triplets.

b. 8 does not fit the pattern. The pattern is plus 1, then times 2. For example, 2 plus 1 equals 3, 3 times 2 equals 6.

Solution

1-800-367-6284

Here is a diagram to help you.

1	2 ABC	3 DEF
4 GHI	5 JKL	6 MNO
7 PQRS	8 TUV	9 WXYZ
*	0	#

Workout #33

And the Answer Is?

Two football teams, the Cougars and the Titans, played each other for the championship. The scores for each team are given below. Who won the game? (Hint: touchdown = 6 points, field goal = 3 points, safety = 2 points, 2-point conversion = 2 points, extra point = 1 point)

Cougars	**Titans**
Touchdown	Field Goal
Extra Point	Field Goal
Touchdown	Field Goal
Extra Point	Field Goal
Field Goal	Touchdown
Safety	2-Point Conversion
Field Goal	Field Goal
Field Goal	Touchdown
Touchdown	Extra Point
2-Point Conversion	Field Goal

Workout #34

Nine Lives

How many total nines
are there between 1 and 100?

Solution #33

It's a tie!
(33 to 33)

Cougars	Titans
6 Touchdown	3 Field Goal
1 Extra Point	3 Field Goal
6 Touchdown	3 Field Goal
1 Extra Point	3 Field Goal
3 Field Goal	6 Touchdown
2 Safety	2-Point Conversion
3 Field Goal	3 Field Goal
3 Field Goal	6 Touchdown
6 Touchdown	1 Extra Point
2-Point Conversion	3 Field Goal
33	33

Solution #34

20

9, 19, 29, 39,
49, 59, 69, 79,
89, 90, 91, 92,
93, 94, 95, 96,
97, 98 and 99

Workout #35

Golf, Anyone?

Golf holes are described as Par 3s, Par 4s and Par 5s. Par is the standard score set for each hole. An eagle is 2 strokes less than par. A birdie is 1 stroke less than par. A bogey is one stroke more than par. A double bogey is two strokes more than par.

Directions: Determine the number of strokes per hole and the total score for the nine holes.

Holes	Par	Score	# of Strokes
1	4	par	?
2	4	bogey	?
3	3	birdie	?
4	4	par	?
5	5	double bogey	?
6	4	par	?
7	3	bogey	?
8	4	birdie	?
9	5	eagle	?
Total	36		Total?

Workout #36

U$A

Directions: Match the denomination with the correct person's portrait.

__ $1 bill   a. Benjamin Franklin

__ $2 bill   b. Ulysses S. Grant

__ $5 bill   c. Alexander Hamilton

__ $10 bill   d. Andrew Jackson

__ $20 bill   e. Thomas Jefferson

__ $50 bill   f. Abraham Lincoln

__ $100 bill   g. George Washington

Holes	Par	Score	# of Strokes
1	4	par	4
2	4	bogey	5
3	3	birdie	2
4	4	par	4
5	5	double bogey	7
6	4	par	4
7	3	bogey	4
8	4	birdie	3
9	5	eagle	3
Total	36		Total 36

Par is an excellent score! Good work!

Solution

The answers are:

g.	$1 bill	George Washington
e.	$2 bill	Thomas Jefferson
f.	$5 bill	Abraham Lincoln
c.	$10 bill	Alexander Hamilton
d.	$20 bill	Andrew Jackson
b.	$50 bill	Ulysses S. Grant
a.	$100 bill	Benjamin Franklin

Let's Go Bowling

The following symbols are used to score bowling:

X = Strike (10 points plus the number of pins knocked down on the next two rolls)

/ = Spare (10 points plus the number of pins knocked down on the next roll)

— = 0 points

Example

(7 + 0)	2	(10 + 6)	3	(6 + 3)	4	(10 + 5 + 2)	5	(5 + 2)
7 —		8 /		6 3		X		5 2
7		23		32		49		56

Directions: Score the following game of bowling.

	2		3		4		5
5 4	6 /		7 1		X		6 2

	7		8		9		10
8 —	9 /		X		5 4		8 1

What's in a Name?

If each letter of the alphabet corresponds with a number,

(A = 1, B = 2, C = 3 . . .)

what is the "value" of your first name? _____

Solution #37

125

Here's how it works:

1	2	3	4	5
5 4	6 /	7 1	X	6 2
9	26	34	52	60

6	7	8	9	10
8 –	9 /	X	5 4	8 1
68	88	107	116	125

Solution #38

Answers will vary.

For example: Ben is worth 21 points.

$$2(B) + 5(E) + 14(N) = 21$$

Who in your class has the highest name value?

Lottery

Workout #39

rections: Choose any three numbers from 0 to 9. Compare your numbers with the winning mber that will follow.

e winning amounts are:

    3 correct numbers—$100
    2 correct numbers—$50
    1 correct number—$10
    0 correct numbers—$0

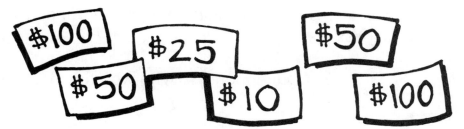

hat is the probability of getting three correct numbers in any order? _____

- -

Workout #40

Unscramble

Unscramble the following letters to make two words:

o w t r o d s w

Then try this one: m p a m b t r o h e l

The winning numbers are 6, 7, 9 (in any order).

The probability of getting three correct numbers is low—1 in 120. There are 120 combinations that you could have selected, and the answer is one of those combinations.

Did you win any fun money? Who won the most money in your class?

Solution

The answers are:

two words

and

math problem

Touchdown

A football team begins play with the ball on the 50-yard line. The team loses 20 yards, gains 10 yards, loses 5 yards and then gains 25 yards. Where are they now?

Workout #41

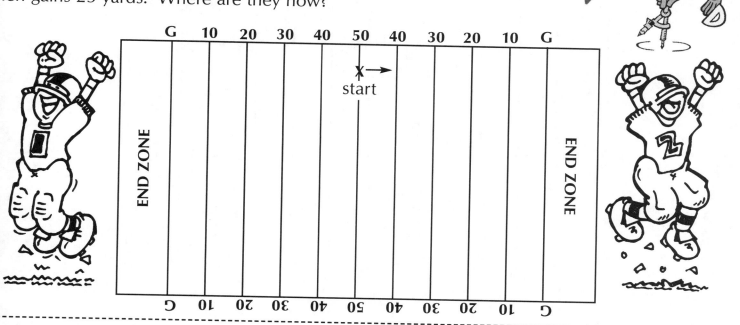

Let's Make Some Music

Workout #42

4/4 musical time, there are four beats in each measure. The notes below have the following number of beats:

1/2 Beat	1 Beat	1 1/2 Beats	2 Beats	3 Beats	4 Beats
♪	♩	♩.	♪	♩.	○

Directions: Divide the music composition below into measures of four beats.

For example, 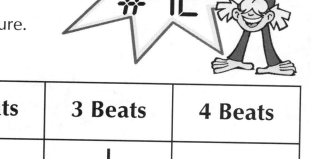 is one measure.

The opposing team's 40-yard line.

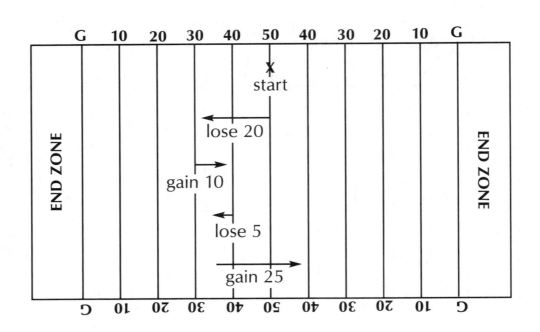

The answer is:

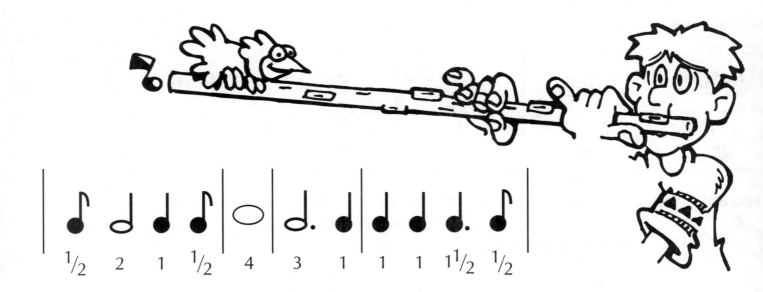

Tick Tock

Directions: Using two straight lines, divide the face of the clock into three parts. The sum of the numbers in each part must be 26.

A Race to the Finish

At the end of a race, Jill is 15 meters behind Will.
Will is 5 meters ahead of Bill.
Bill is 15 meters ahead of Phil.
Phil is 5 meters behind Jill.
In what order did they finish the race?

1. _____

2. _____

3. _____

4. _____

The answer is:

Solution #44

1. Will   2. Bill   3. Jill   4. Phil

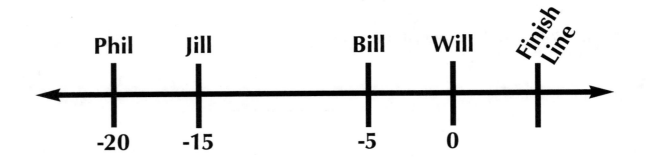

Bull's-Eye

Workout #45

Directions: Place five darts on the dartboard to get a score of exactly 24?

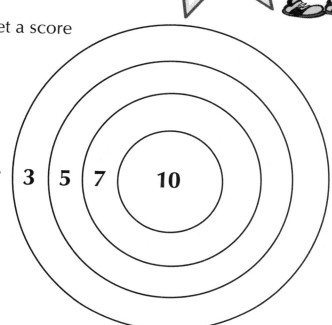

3 5 7 10

- -

UNIT 4 Math Concepts, Analysis and Computation

Math Symbols

Workout #46

Match the correct math symbols.

_____ ≠   a. equal to
_____ %   b. not equal to
_____ Σ   c. less than or equal to
_____ π   d. percent
_____ =   e. sum of certain terms
_____ ≤   f. plus or minus
_____ >   g. approximately
_____ ≈   h. circumference divided by diameter
_____ ±   i. greater than

Solution #45

The answer is:

3 — 3 pointers   9
1 — 10 pointer 10
1 — 5 pointer   <u>5</u>
Total: 24 points

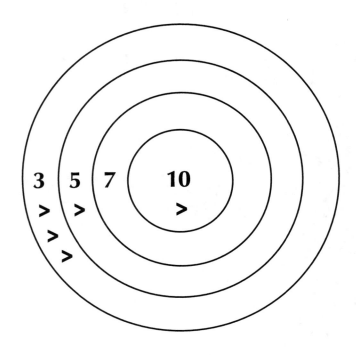

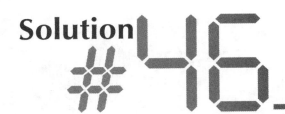

Solution #46

The answers are:

b	≠	b. not equal to
d	%	d. percent
e	Σ	e. sum of certain terms
h	π	h. circumference divided by diameter
a	=	a. equal to
c	≤	c. less than or equal to
i	>	i. greater than
g	≈	g. approximately
f	±	f. plus or minus

Fun with Divisibility

Note:
A number is divisible by three if the sum of its digits is divisible by three.
A number is divisible by six if the number is even and the sum of its digits is divisible by three.
A number is divisible by nine if the sum of its digits is divisible by nine.

Directions: Determine if the following numbers are divisible by 3, 6 and/or 9:

a. 111

b. 621

c. 732

d. 8,303

e. 7,704

UNIT 4 **Math Concepts, Analysis and Computation**
Binary Notation

Binary notation is a number system that uses Base 2 instead of Base 10. Base 10 is the system we are familiar with. It uses digits 1 through 9. Base 2 only uses the digits 0 and 1. The place value system for Base 2 is as follows:

2^6	2^5	2^4	2^3	2^2	2^1	2^0
64	32	16	8	4	2	1
				1	0	1
			1	1	1	0

When there is a 1 in Base 2, you add that number. When there is a 0, you don't add anything. For example, 101 in Base 2 equals 5 (1 + 0 + 4). 1110 in Base 2 equals 14 (0 + 2 + 4 + 8).

Directions: Using the table above, convert the following numbers from Base 2 to Base 10:

a. 1 _____   b. 110 _____   c. 1010 _____   d. 10001 _____   e. 1100100 _____

The answers are:

a. 111—divisible by 3
b. 621—divisible by 3 and 9
c. 732—divisible by 3 and 6
d. 8,303—none
e. 7,704—divisible by 3, 6 and 9

The answers are:

a. 11 = 3
b. 110 = 6
c. 1010 = 10
d. 10001 = 17
e. 1100100 = 100

2^6	2^5	2^4	2^3	2^2	2^1	2^0
64	32	16	8	4	2	1
					1	1
				1	1	0
			1	0	1	0
		1	0	0	0	1
1	1	0	0	1	0	0

56

Branches of Mathematics

Can you correctly match these branches of mathematics with their descriptions?

___ Algebra ___ Calculus ___ Geometry ___ Statistics ___ Trigonometry

- a branch of mathematics that deals with measurement of angles, lines, points, solids and surfaces
- a branch of mathematics that deals with applications of functions like sine, cosine and tangent
- a branch of mathematics that uses symbols (letters/variables) to solve problems
- a branch of higher mathematics that deals with differentiation and integration of functions
- a branch of mathematics that deals with data collection, analysis and interpretation

---

UNIT 4 **Math Concepts, Analysis and Computation**

Absolute Value

Absolute value is the unit value a number is from zero on the number line. The symbol for absolute value is two vertical lines (| |).

Example: $|5| = 5$ and $|-5| = 5$. Absolute value is positive except in the case of $|0| = 0$.

Answer the following:

$|-8| = $ _____

$|{}^3/_4|$ _____

$|-9| + |12|$ _____

$|3 - 5|$ _____

Solution #49

The answers are:

a. Algebra
b. Calculus
c. Geometry
d. Statistics
e. Trigonometry

Geometry is a branch of mathematics that deals with the measurement of angles, lines, points, solids and surfaces.

Trigonometry is a branch of mathematics that deals with applications of functions like sine, cosine and tangent.

Algebra is a branch of mathematics that us symbols (letters/variables) to solve problem

Calculus is a branch of higher mathematics th deals with differentiation and integration functions.

Statistics is a branch of mathematics that de with data collection, analysis and interpretatic

Solution #50

The answers are:

a. $|-8| = 8$

b. $|^3/_4| = {}^3/_4$

c. $|-9| + |12| = 9 + 12 = 21$

d. $|3 - 5| = |-2| = 2$

58

Quadrants

rectangular coordinate system is divided into four parts
lled quadrants.

rections: Identify the quadrants of
e following points. If the point is on
axis, indicate which axis.

(-3,6) _____

(-2,-1) _____

(0,-2) _____

(-4,5) _____

($^1/_2$, 4) _____

(-8, 0) _____

(.75, $^{-5}/_4$) _____

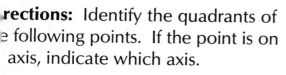

II

I

$-$

$+$

II

I

III

IV

y

x

ID Required

tch the following math terms and operations:

___ 1. divisor   ___ 6. minuend

___ 2. addends   ___ 7. factors

___ 3. product   ___ 8. difference

___ 4. dividend   ___ 9. quotient

___ 5. subtrahend   ___ 10. sum

503 (a)
+16 (a)
─────
519 (b)

782 (f)
- 61 (g)
─────
621 (h)

$225 \div 25 = 5$
(c) (d) (e)

$25 \times 5 = 125$
(i) (i) (j)

The answers are:

In quadrant I, the x and y coordinates are both positive. In quadrant II, the x coordinate is negative and the y coordinate is positive. In quadrant III, the x and y coordinates are both negative. In quadrant IV, the x coordinate is positive and the y coordinate is negative. A point is on the x axis when the y coordinate is 0. A point is on the y axis when the x coordinate is 0.

	II	I
	(−,+)	(+,+)
	III	IV
	(−,−)	(+,−)

a. (-3,6)   II
b. (-2,-1)   III
c. (0,-2)   y axis
d. (-4,5)   II
e. ($\frac{1}{2}$,4)   I
f. (-8,0)   x axis
g. (.75,$^{-5}/_4$)   IV

Solution #52

The answers are:

1. divisor = d
2. addends = a
3. product = j
4. dividend = c
5. subtrahend = g
6. minuend = f
7. factors = i
8. difference = h
9. quotient = e
10. sum = b

Great Graphs

aph the following points and connect with line segments:

(4,2)   (4,4)   (2,4)   (0,4)   (-2,4)   (-4,4)   (-4,2)   (-4,0)

(-4,-2)   (-4,-4)   (-2,-4)   (0,-4)   (2,-4)   (4,-4)   (4,-2)   (4,0)

t your pencil after you connect the points. Now graph (2,3), (-2,3) Do **not** connect these points.

w graph and connect in order:

(-2,-2)   (-1,-3)   (0,-3)   (1,-3)   (2,-2)

NIT 4 **Math Concepts, Analysis and Computation**

Go Metric!

me the appropriate metric unit to measure the following:

____ 1. The amount of gas in your gas tank

____ 2. The temperature outside

____ 3. The distance from New York to Chicago

____ 4. The length of a football field

____ 5. Your weight

____ 6. The thickness of a dime

____ 7. The length of a sheet of notebook paper

____ 8. The mass of your pencil

Smile!

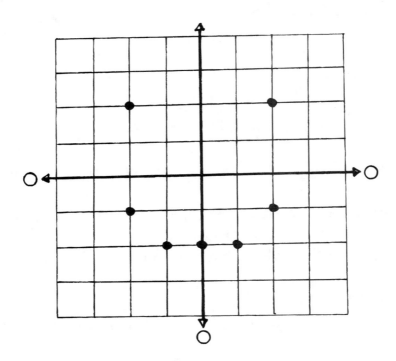

Solution #54

The answers are:

liters (L)

Celsius (C)

kilometers (km)

meters (m)

kilograms (kg)

millimeters (mm)

centimeters (cm)

grams (g)

1. The amount of gas in your gas tank
2. The temperature outside
3. The distance from New York to Chicago
4. The length of a football field
5. Your weight
6. The thickness of a dime
7. The length of a sheet of notebook paper
8. The mass of your pencil

Helpful Hints

Weight/Mass
grams: used to measure light objects
kilograms: used like the pound
Distance/Length
mm: about the thickness of a dime
cm: used like the inch
m: used like the yard
km: used like the mile
Volume/Capacity
milliliter: capacity of small objects like an eyedropp
liter: used like the quart/gallon
Temperature
Celsius: commonly used to measure temperature

Domain and Range

In a set of ordered pairs, the **domain** is made up of the x-coordinates and are considered independent variables. The **range** is made up of the y-coordinates and are considered the dependent variables. The domain and range of a set are generally listed in order from least to greatest.

Directions: List the domain and range for the following sets of ordered pairs:

(2,4) (3,6) (4,8) (5,10) = domain _____ range _____

(-2,-1) (8,4) (7,3.5) (-6,-3) = domain _____ range _____

(0,1) (1,3) (2,5) (3,7) = domain _____ range _____

Choose an Appropriate Graph

Directions: Match the type of graph with its appropriate use.

Scatter Plot _____

Bar Graph _____

Line Graph _____

Circle Graph _____

Stem-and-Leaf Plot _____

Box-and-Whisker Graph _____

1. Compares parts to a whole

2. Shows correlation

3. Shows the distribution of data

4. Compares data

5. Distributes data around the median

6. Shows changes in data

The answers are:

a. (2,4) (3,6) (4,8) (5,10)
   domain = {2,3,4,5}
   range = {4,6,8,10}

b. (-2,-1) (8,4) (7,3.5) (-6,-3)
   domain = {-6,-2,7,8}
   range   = {-3,-1,3.5,4}

c. (0,1) (1,3) (2,5) (3,7)
   domain = {0,1,2,3}
   range   = {1,3,5,7}

Solution

a. 2; b. 4; c. 6; d. 1; e. 4; f. 5; c. (

1. Circle Graph: compares parts to a whole

2. Scatter Plot: shows correlation

3. Stem-and-Leaf Plot: shows the distribution of data

4. Bar Graph: compares data

5. Box-and-Whisker Graph: distributes data around the median

6. Line Graph: shows changes in data

Workout #57

Order, Please

Solve the following problems. Be sure to pay attention to the order of operations.

$6 + 12 \div 3 - 2 \times 5 =$ _____

$4 \div 2^2 \times (5 - 3) =$ _____

$(3 + 2)^2 + 9 \div 3 =$ _____

UNIT 4 **Math Concepts, Analysis and Computation**

What's in a Graph?

Workout #58

Bar graphs are used to show data comparisons.
Line graphs are used to show changes in data.
Circle graphs are used to show parts of a whole.

Directions: Choose the most appropriate graph to display the following:

___ 1. high temperatures for a region throughout the year

___ 2. how a student spends his or her allowance

___ 3. school attendance between boys and girls

___ 4. your height for the past eight years

___ 5. the student enrollment at five different middle schools

___ 6. the amount of time each day spent on various activities
   (e.g. school, sleeping, homework, watching television)

a. 0; b. 2; c. 28

In order to have uniform answers, you must follow a certain order when working math problems. The order of operations is as follows:

1. Perform operations inside the parentheses first.

2. Simplify your exponents.

3. Multiply or divide from left to right.

4. Add or subtract from left to right.

For example: $(3 + 2)^2 + 9 \div 3$

1. Simplify inside your parentheses $(3 + 2) = 5$.

2. Simplify the exponent $(5^2) = 25$.

3. Divide $(9 \div 3) = 3$.

4. Add $(25 + 3) = 28$.

Solution

The answers are:

1. b. Line graph

2. c. Circle graph

3. a. Bar graph

4. b. Line graph

5. a. Bar graph

6. c. Circle graph

Trying Triangles

Workout
#59

The sum of the interior angles of a triangle is always equal to 180°.
Find the measure of the missing angle.

a. 30°, 60°, _____

b. 45°, 90°, _____

c. 20°, 55°, _____

d. 15°, 70°, _____

When in Rome

Workout
#60

man Numerals: a system for writing integers used in Ancient Rome.

I = 1   V = 5   X = 10   L = 50   C = 100   D = 500   M = 1000

sic rule: When a letter of lesser value comes before a greater number the values are subtracted (IV = 4).

ections: Translate the following Roman numerals:

a. VII _____   d. DCC _____

b. IX _____   e. MM _____

c. XL _____   f. MMIX _____

Solution #59

a. 90°; b. 45°; c. 105°; d. 95°

a. 30 + 60 = 90   180 – 90 = **90°**

b. 45 + 90 = 135   180 – 135 = **45°**

c. 20 + 55 = 75   180 – 75 = **105°**

d. 15 + 70 = 85   180 – 85 = **95°**

Solution #60

The answers are:

a. VII = 7

b. IX = 9

c. XL = 40

d. DCC = 700

e. MM = 2000

f. MMIX = 2009

Prime vs. Composite

A **prime** number is a whole number whose only factors are itself and 1. A **composite** number has more than two factors.

Directions: Circle the prime numbers in the following list:

1	4	8	51	26
111	99	47	2	5
57	69	6	39	19
87	9	37	59	13
7	41	3	33	27
81	12	67	11	29

Palindromes

A palindrome is a number that is the same when you read it from left to right or right to left. For example, 121 is a palindrome.

Directions: List all of the palindromes greater than 20 and less than 120.

There are 13 prime numbers in the list.

1	4	8	51	26
111	99	(47)	(2)	(5)
57	69	6	39	(19)
87	9	(37)	(59)	(13)
(7)	(41)	(3)	33	27
81	12	(67)	(11)	(29)

Note: 1 is neither prime nor composite.

Solution #62

The answers are:

22, 33, 44,
55, 66, 77, 88,
99, 101, 111

Prime Factorization

ime **factorization** is expressing a number as a product
only prime numbers.

amples
= 2 x 3 x 5
= 3 x 3 x 2

press the following numbers using prime factorization:

a. 25 _____

b. 48 _____

c. 72 _____

d. 120 _____

e. 200 _____

Trigonometric Ratios

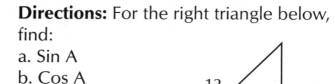

gonometric **ratios** are ratios of the lengths of the
es of a right triangle.

$$e\ (Sin) = \frac{opposite}{hypotenuse}$$ $$Cosine\ (Cos) = \frac{adjacent}{hypotenuse}$$ $$Tangent\ (Tan) = \frac{opposite}{adjacent}$$

ample:

$$in\ A = \frac{4}{5}$$

$$os\ A = \frac{3}{5}$$

$$an\ A = \frac{4}{3}$$

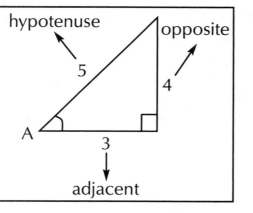

hypotenuse

opposite

5

4

A

3

adjacent

Directions: For the right triangle below,
find:
a. Sin A
b. Cos A
c. Tan A

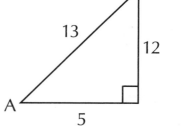

13

12

A

5

The answers are:

Note: The factors can be written in any order.

a. $25 = 5 \times 5$
b. $48 = 2 \times 2 \times 2 \times 2 \times 3$
c. $72 = 3 \times 3 \times 2 \times 2 \times 2$
d. $120 = 5 \times 3 \times 2 \times 2 \times 2$
e. $200 = 5 \times 5 \times 2 \times 2 \times 2$

The answers are:

$$\text{Sin } A = \frac{12}{13}$$

$$\text{Cos } A = \frac{5}{13}$$

$$\text{Tan } A = \frac{12}{5}$$

Multiples vs. Factors

Workout #65

Multiples are products of a number. For example, some multiples of 8 are 8, 16, 24, 32, 40 and 48.

Factors are divisors. For example, the factors of 24 are 1, 2, 4, 6, 8, 12 and 24.

Directions: List the factors and the first six multiples of 18 and 27. Identify the Greatest Common Factor (GCF) and the Least Common Multiple (LCM) of the two numbers.

18

factors _____

multiples _____

27

factors _____

multiples _____

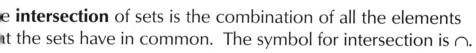

Sensational Sets

Workout #66

The **union** of sets is the combination of all the elements in the sets. The symbol for union is ∪.

The **intersection** of sets is the combination of all the elements that the sets have in common. The symbol for intersection is ∩.

Given: A = {0, 1, 2, 3, 4, 5}
         B = {6, 7, 8, 9, 10}
         C = {1, 3, 5, 7}

Find: 1. A ∪ B
        2. B ∩ C
        3. B ∪ C
        4. A ∩ B

Solution #65

The answers are:

Factors
18—1, 2, 3, 6, 9, 18
27—1, 3, 9, 27
GCF = 9

Multiples
18—18, 36, 54, 72, 90, 108
27—27, 54, 81, 108, 135, 162
LCM = 54

Solution #66

The answers are:

1. $A \cup B = \{0, 1, 2, 3, 4, 5, 6, 7, 8, 9, 10\}$

2. $B \cap C = \{7\}$

3. $B \cup C = \{1, 3, 5, 6, 7, 8, 9, 10\}$

4. $A \cap B = \varnothing$ or $\{\ \}$

74

Stem-and-Leaf Plots

Workout #67

tem-and-leaf plots are used to show how data is distributed.
he numbers 8, 15, 19, 22, 27, 29, 32, 38, 40 give a mound
hape when shown in the stem-and-leaf plot below.

o create a stem-and-leaf plot, use the range of the left digits of each number to form the stems
nd the right digits to make the leaf. For example, 2|2 7 9 refers to 22, 27 and 29.

```
  | 8
  | 5 9
  | 2 7 9
  | 2 8
  | 0
```

irections: Develop a stem-and-leaf plot to display the following numbers:
34, 49, 33, 70, 55, 61, 43, 40, 52, 53, 61, 77, 53, 68

- -

Triangular Area

Workout #68

e area of a triangle is equal to $\frac{1}{2}$ its base times its height
$= \frac{1}{2}$ BH).

d the area of the following triangles:

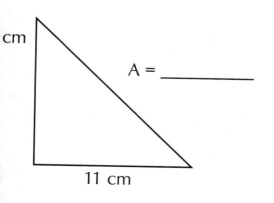

cm

A = _____

11 cm

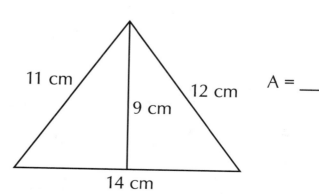

11 cm   12 cm
9 cm

A = _____

14 cm

The answer is:

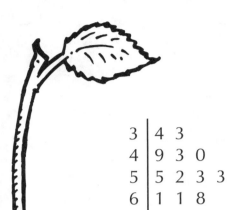

```
3 | 4 3
4 | 9 3 0
5 | 5 2 3 3
6 | 1 1 8
7 | 0 7
```

Or in numerical order:

```
3 | 3 4
4 | 0 3 9
5 | 2 3 3 5
6 | 1 1 8
7 | 0 7
```

This stem-and-leaf plot also has a mound shape distribution pattern—
most of the numbers are in the middle.

Solution #68

44 cm² and 63 cm²

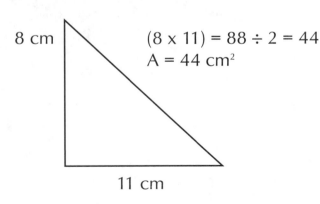

8 cm

$(8 \times 11) = 88 \div 2 = 44$
$A = 44 \text{ cm}^2$

11 cm

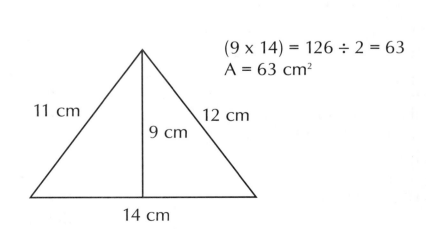

$(9 \times 14) = 126 \div 2 = 63$
$A = 63 \text{ cm}^2$

11 cm

12 cm

9 cm

14 cm

Digging for Square Roots

Workout #69

A **square root** of a number is a number which, when multiplied by itself, produces the given number. So the $\sqrt{4}$ is 2 because 2 x 2 = 4. The symbol for a square root is the radical ($\sqrt{}$).

Directions: Find the square roots of the following numbers:

$\sqrt{9}$ = _____

$\sqrt{36}$ = _____

$\sqrt{144}$ = _____

$\sqrt{81}$ = _____

$\sqrt{625}$ = _____

$\sqrt{10,000}$ = _____

Pascal's Triangle

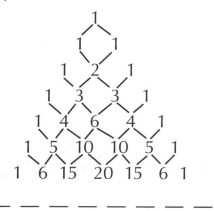

Workout #70

Pascal's Triangle can help you find probabilities. Here are the steps for constructing Pascal's Triangle:

Start with a triangle of three 1s in the first two rows.
Each row should contain one more number than the number of rows.
Each row must begin and end with a 1.
Each number in the triangle is the sum of the two numbers above it.

Directions: Complete row 7 and row 8.

Row 0   1
Row 1   1   1
Row 2   1   2   1
Row 3   1   3   3   1
Row 4   1   4   6   4   1
Row 5   1   5 10 10   5   1
Row 6 1   6 15 20 15   6   1
Row 7 __ __ __ __ __ __ __ __
Row 8 __ __ __ __ __ __ __ __ __

Solution #69

The answers are:

$$\sqrt{9} = 3$$

$$\sqrt{36} = 6$$

$$\sqrt{144} = 12$$

$$\sqrt{81} = 9$$

$$\sqrt{625} = 25$$

$$\sqrt{10,000} = 100$$

Solution #70

The answers are:

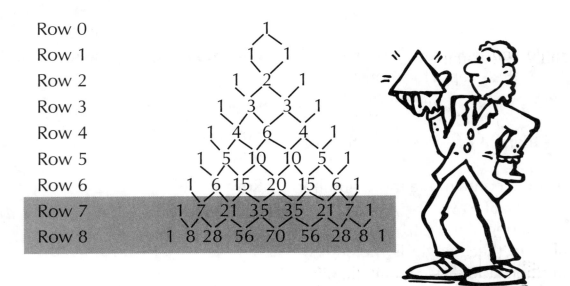

Row 0	1
Row 1	1 1
Row 2	1 2 1
Row 3	1 3 3 1
Row 4	1 4 6 4 1
Row 5	1 5 10 10 5 1
Row 6	1 6 15 20 15 6 1
Row 7	1 7 21 35 35 21 7 1
Row 8	1 8 28 56 70 56 28 8 1

Deal Me In

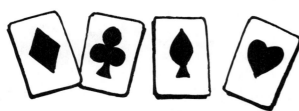

Your friend asks you to randomly pick a card from a regular deck of cards.
What are the odds that you will pick the king of clubs?
What is the probability that you will pick a spade or a diamond?
What are the chances that you will pick a heart?
Remember, there are 52 cards in a deck.

King of Clubs = _____

Spade/Diamond = _____

Heart = _____

Unit 4 Math Concepts, Analysis and Computation

A Fact of the Circle

circle has 360°. Determine the number of degrees in the following fractions of a circle:

a. $\frac{1}{2}$ = _____

b. $\frac{3}{4}$ = _____

c. $\frac{1}{9}$ = _____

d. $\frac{2}{3}$ = _____

e. $\frac{5}{6}$ = _____

Solution #71

The answers are:

King of Clubs: There is a $\frac{1}{52}$ chance of picking the king of clubs because there is only one king of clubs in a standard 52-card deck.

Spade/Diamond: There is a $\frac{1}{2}$ chance of picking either a spade or a diamond because there are 13 spades and 13 diamonds in the deck. These 26 cards make up half of the deck.

Heart: There is a $\frac{1}{4}$ chance of picking a heart because 13 of the 52 cards in the deck are hearts.

Solution #72

The answers are:

a. $\frac{1}{2} \times \frac{360}{1} = 180°$

b. $\frac{3}{4} \times \frac{360}{1} = 270°$

c. $\frac{1}{9} \times \frac{360}{1} = 40°$

d. $\frac{2}{3} \times \frac{360}{1} = 240°$

e. $\frac{5}{6} \times \frac{360}{1} = 300°$

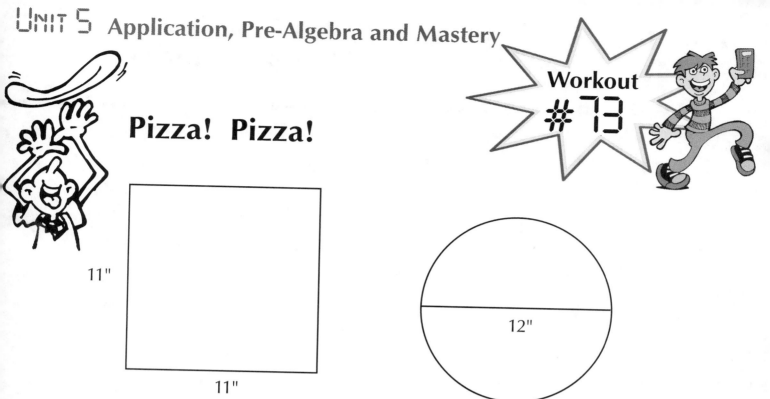

Pizza! Pizza!

Workout #73

11"

11"

12"

You and a friend are ordering a pizza. Assuming you want to get the most pizza, should you order the 12" round or the 11" square pizza? Both pizzas are the same price.

Workout #74

Working Wages

Luis has a job that pays $5.00 an hour for the first 40 hours worked in a week; pays 1.5 times his hourly wage for any time over that. Luis worked 52 hours last week. How much will his paycheck be?

Solution #73

11" square pizza

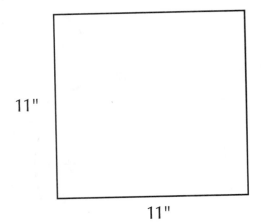

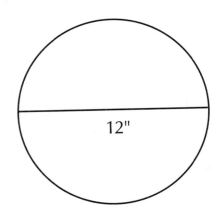

A = l x w
  = 11 x 11
  = 121 in²

A = 3.14 x r²
  = 3.14 x 6²
  = 3.14 x 36
  = 113.04 in²

Solution #74

$290

Regular pay   = $200
(40 hours x $5)

Overtime pay   = $ 90
(12 hours x $7.50)
                        $290

1.5 x or "time and a half" equals
regular pay ($5) + ½ of regular pay ($5 x ½ = $2.50).
Luis makes $7.50 per hour for overtime hours.

Everyday Conversions

onvert the following:

3 days = _____ hours

4 minutes = _____ seconds

3 gallons = _____ quarts

2 yards = _____ feet

32 ounces = _____ pints

1 mile = _____ yards

1 mile = _____ feet

2 pounds = _____ ounces

Honor Roll

nifer hopes to make the honor roll. At her school,
needs a 3.0 grade point average to make the
nor roll. Here is Jennifer's report card:

Science	A
French	C
English	B
P.E.	A
Social Studies	D
Math	A
Band	B

ed on a four-point scale (A = 4, B = 3, C = 2, D = 1, F = 0), does Jennifer make the honor roll?

Solution #75

The answers are:

3 days = 72 hours

4 minutes = 240 seconds

3 gallons = 12 quarts

2 yards = 6 feet

32 ounces = 2 pints

1 mile = 1760 yards

1 mile = 5280 feet

2 pounds = 32 ounces

Solution #76

Jennifer made the honor roll!

Add up the grade values, and divide by the number of subjects (7) to find her grade point average.

Science	A	4
French	C	2
English	B	3
P.E.	A	4
Social Studies	D	1
Math	A	4
Band	B	3

$$4 + 2 + 3 + 4 + 1 + 4 + 3 = 21$$
$$21 \div 7 = 3$$

Tricky

What is 10 divided by $\frac{1}{2}$

and then added to three? _____

An Age-Old Question

Lisa is twice as old as Leroy.
Luther is twice as old as Lisa.
The sum of all three ages is 28.
How old are Lisa, Leroy and Luther?

23

Remember that when you divide by a fraction such as $\frac{1}{2}$, you must multiply by its reciprocal.

$$10 \div \frac{1}{2} = 10 \times \frac{2}{1} = 20$$

$$20 + 3 = 23$$

Solution

Leroy is 4; Lisa is 8 and Luther is 16.

Explanation

Let x represent the youngest person's (Leroy) age, then 2x represents Lisa's age, and 4x represents Luther's age.

$$x + 2x + 4x = 28$$
$$7x = 28$$
$$x = 4$$

Leroy (x) = 4 years old

Lisa (2x or 2 x 4) = 8 years old

Luther (4x or 4 x 4) = 16 years old

Solving Equations

order to solve basic equations for x, you must cancel terms performing the opposite operation. Division and multiplition are opposite operations. Addition and subtraction are posite operations.

ections: Identify the correct procedures to solve the following problems:

___ 1. $x + 5 = 12$ a. divide by 5

___ 2. $x - 5 = 12$ b. subtract 5

___ 3. $5x = 30$ c. multiply by 5

___ 4. $\frac{x}{5} = 9$ d. add 5, then divide by 5

___ 5. $5x - 5 = 10$ e. add 5

Shopping with Leah

At the mall, Leah purchased a jacket for $29.95
and a pair of tennis shoes for $27.50.
Where she lives, she must pay a 6% sales tax.
What was the total cost of Leah's purchase, including tax?

$ _____.____

The answers are:

b. subtract 5—1. $x + 5 = 12$

e. add 5—2. $x - 5 = 12$

a. divide by 5—3. $5x = 30$

c. multiply by 5—4. $\frac{x}{5} = 9$

d. add 5, then divide by 5—5. $5x - 5 = 10$

Solution

$60.90

Explanation

Add the two purchases together.

$29.95—jacket
+ $27.50—shoes
  $57.45

Next, calculate the amount of sales tax (6% of $57.45).

To do this, change 6% to a decimal (.06) and multiply by $57.45.

$57.45
x   .06
$ 3.447 $\cong$ $3.45

Then, add the sales tax to the price of the items to get the total cost.

$57.45
+ $ 3.45
  $60.90

Like Signs

Workout
#81

hen adding like signs (positive plus positive or negative plus negative), simply add the absolute
ues of the numbers and keep the sign for your sum.

amples
- 9 = 17
+ (-9) = -17

rections: Add the following:

a. -7 + (-3) = _____   c. .25 + .05 = _____

b. -$\frac{1}{2}$ + (-4) = _____   d. -1 + (-.28) = _____

Squaring a Number Ending in 5

Workout
#82

uaring any two-digit number ending in 5 is easy. Just
member, the product will always end with 25 and to get
first or first two digits, multiply the number in the tens
umn by one more than that number [n x (n + 1)].

example, 35^2 = 1225 (multiply 3 times 4 [3 + 1] which equals 12).

rections: Compute the following quickly with the shortcut. No calculators please.

1. 25^2 _____   3. 75^2 _____

2. 15^2 _____   4. 95^2 _____

The answers are:

a. -7 + (-3) = -10

b. $-^1/_2 + (-4) = -4^1/_2$

c. .25 + .05 = .30

d. -1 + (-.28) = -1.28

Solution #82

The answers are:

1. $25^2 = 625$ (2 x 3 = 6, thus 625)

2. $15^2 = 225$ (1 x 2 = 2, thus 225)

3. $75^2 = 5625$ (7 x 8 = 56, thus 5625)

4. $95^2 = 9025$ (9 x 10 = 90, thus 9025)

M and M and Ms

Find the **mean**, **mode** and **median** of the following set of numbers:

22, 24, 11, 7, 32, 24

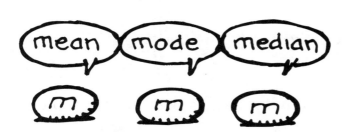

Mean = _____

Mode = _____

Median = _____

Awesome Angles

Complementary angles are two angles whose measures add up to 90°. For example, a 40° and a 50° angle are complementary.

Supplementary angles are two angles whose measures add up to 180°. For example, a 120° and a 60° angle are supplementary.

Find the angle's complement.

30° _____

45° _____

55° _____

89° _____

Find the angle's supplement.

e. 100° _____

f.   20° _____

g.   45° _____

h. 116° _____

Solution #83

The answers are:

Mean = 20
Mode = 24
Median = 23

The **mean** is the same as the average. Add the numbers, and then divide by the number of numbers in the group $(22 + 24 + 11 + 7 + 32 + 24) \div 6 = 20$.

The **mode** is the number than occurs with the highest frequency (24). There can be more than one mode.

The **median** is the middle number of a set that is arranged in numerical order. In order, the numbers are 7, 11, 22, 24, 24, 32. When there is an even number in the set, two numbers will appear in the middle (22, 24). When that happens, find the average of the two numbers $(22 + 24) \div 2 = 23$.

Solution #84

The answers are:

a. $90° - 30° = 60°$

b. $90° - 45° = 45°$

c. $90° - 55° = 35°$

d. $90° - 89° = 1°$

e. $180° - 100° = 80°$

f. $180° - 20° = 160°$

g. $180° - 45° = 135°$

h. $180° - 116° = 64°$

Workout #85

Exponential Notation

Directions: Write each of the following in exponential notation.

Example: $2 \times 2 \times 3 \times 3 \times 3 = 2^2 \times 3^3$

$3 \times 3 \times 3 \times 7 \times 7$ _____

$5 \times 2 \times 3 \times 5 \times 3 \times 3$ _____

$2 \times 11 \times 11 \times 2 \times 2 \times 11$ _____

$2 \times 7 \times 11 \times 2 \times 2 \times 2 \times 7 \times 11 \times 3$ _____

$5 \times 5 \times 2 \times 3 \times 3 \times 5 \times 5 \times 2 \times 3$ _____

- -

UNIT 5 Application, Pre-Algebra and Mastery

Workout #86

You Deserve a Raise!

Andrew works weekends at the
local grocery store for $6.70 per hour.
Because Andrew does such a good job,
the manager of the store is going
to is give Andrew a 10% raise.
What will Andrew's new
hourly wage be after the raise?

$_____.____

Solution #85

The answers are:

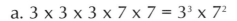

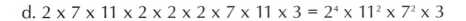

a. $3 \times 3 \times 3 \times 7 \times 7 = 3^3 \times 7^2$

b. $5 \times 2 \times 3 \times 5 \times 3 \times 3 = 5^2 \times 3^3 \times 2$

c. $2 \times 11 \times 11 \times 2 \times 2 \times 11 = 11^3 \times 2^3$

d. $2 \times 7 \times 11 \times 2 \times 2 \times 2 \times 7 \times 11 \times 3 = 2^4 \times 11^2 \times 7^2 \times 3$

e. $5 \times 5 \times 2 \times 3 \times 3 \times 5 \times 5 \times 2 \times 3 = 5^4 \times 3^3 \times 2^2$

*The exponential notations can be listed in any order.

Solution #86

$7.37 per hour

Here's how:

10% of $6.70 =
(.1 x 6.70) = $0.67

$6.70
+ 0.67
$7.37

94

More or Less?

Place the correct symbol <, > or = in the equations below.

a. 2.07 _____ 2.1

b. .25 _____ .206

c. .1304 _____ .13038

d. .705_____ .7050

e. 10.90008 _____ 10.9807

Computer Terms

Match the terms with the definitions below:

___ e-mail   ___ monitor   ___ Internet

___ cyberspace   ___ printer   ___ modem

an imaginary place where virtual objects appear

message sent electronically from one person to another

a device that links a computer to a phone line

d. a worldwide network of computers used to share information

e. a video display screen for a computer

f. an output device for a computer

Solution #87

The answers are:

a. 2.07 < 2.1
b. .25 > .206
c. .1304 > .13038
d. .705 = .7050
e. 10.90008 < 10.9807

Helpful Hints

There are several ways to work these problems. One way is to place zeros at the end of one of the numbers so that both numbers have the same number of digits after the decimal. Then, remove the decimals and compare the numbers as if they were two whole numbers.

We'll use .1304 and .13038 as an example.

1. Place a zero at the end of .1304 so that both numbers have five digits to the right of the decimal (.13040 and .13038).
2. Remove the decimals and compare the numbers like whole numbers (13,040 and 13,038).
3. 13,040 is greater, so .1304 > .13038.

Solution #88

The answers are:

b. e-mail

e. monitor

d. Internet

a. cyberspace

f. printer

c. modem

Team Relay

The Mathsville's school record in the 400-meter relay is 47.9 seconds.
Jermaine is the anchor on the relay team.
If Jasmine runs her lap in 11.8 seconds,
Jordan runs in 12 seconds and
James runs in 12.3 seconds,
how fast must Jermaine run the final leg
of the race to tie the school record?

_____

More Computer Terms

Match the terms with the definitions below:

_____ hardware   _____ software   _____ network

_____ browser   _____ bit   _____ megabyte

a program used to look at various Internet resources

consists of the printer, modem and disk drives

the smallest computerized data

d. computer programs

e. a million bytes

f. two or more computers connected to shared resources

The answer is:

11.8 seconds

The answers are:

b. hardware

d. software

f. network

a. browser

c. bit

e. megabyte

Unlike Signs

Workout #91

When adding unlike signs, subtract the absolute value of the numbers. Then use the sign of the number with the greatest absolute value in your answer.

Examples
- -5 + 15 = |5| – |15| = 10
- 5 + (-15) = |5| – |15| = -10

Answer the following:

a. -8 + 23 = _____

b. 19 + (-29) = _____

c. -18 + 11 = _____

d. 3.8 + (-1.9) = _____

e. $-\frac{1}{2} + \frac{1}{3}$ = _____

f. -23 + 32 + (-12) = _____

Additive Inverse

Workout #92

The **additive inverse** of a number is its opposite. The additive inverse of a positive number is negative. The additive inverse of a negative number is positive.

Examples
- -(5) = -5
- -(-5) = 5

Answer the following:

-(10) = _____

$-(-\frac{1}{2})$ = _____

c. -(12) + 32 = _____

d. -|4| = _____

e. -|-5| = _____

The answers are:

a. -8 + 23 = 15

b. 19 + (-29) = -10

c. -18 + 11 = -7

d. 3.8 + (-1.9) = 1.9

e. $-\frac{1}{2} + \frac{1}{3} = -\frac{1}{6}$

f. -23 + 32 + (-12) = -3

Solution #92

The answers are:

a. -(10) = -10

b. $-(-\frac{1}{2}) = \frac{1}{2}$

c. -(12) + 32 = 20

d. -|4| = -4

e. -|-5| = -5

Subtracting a New Way

Workout #93

Subtracting is same as adding the additive inverse of a number.

Examples

-5 − 10 = -5 + (-10) = -15

12 − (-23) = 12 + 23 = 25

Answer the following:

a. 10 − 19 = _____

b. -23 − 14 = _____

c. -15 − (-26) = _____

d. 23 − (-21) = _____

e. $^3/_5 − ^7/_{10}$ = _____

Reciprocate, Please!

Workout #94

A **reciprocal** of a number is formed by switching the numerator and denominator.

Name the reciprocals of the following numbers:

a. $^2/_3$ = _____

b. 5 = _____

c. $^1/_9$ = _____

d. $4^6/_7$ = _____

a. $10 - 19 = 10 + (-19) = -9$

b. $-23 - 14 = -23 + (-14) = -37$

c. $-15 - (-26) = -15 + 26 = 11$

d. $23 - (-21) = 23 + 21 = 44$

e. $\frac{3}{5} - \frac{7}{10} = \frac{6}{10} + (-\frac{7}{10}) = -\frac{1}{10}$

Solution  The answers are:

a. $\frac{2}{3} = \frac{3}{2}$

b. 5 or $\frac{5}{1} = \frac{1}{5}$

c. $\frac{1}{9} = 9$ or $\frac{9}{1}$

d. $4\frac{6}{7}$ or $\frac{34}{7} = \frac{7}{34}$

Accentuate the Positive

ubtracting a negative number is the same as adding a positive (its additive inverse). or example, -9 – (-5) is the same as –9 + 5.

nswer the following:

-10 – (-5) = _____   d. 9 – (-18) = _____

12 – (8) = _____   e. 0 – (-18) = _____

-15 – (-23) = _____   f. $\frac{1}{2} - (-\frac{3}{4})$ = _____

Even More Computer Terms

Workout #96

atch the terms with the definitions below:

____ PDA   ____ HTML   ____ home page

____ password   ____ bps (bits-per-second)

a code used to gain access to a locked system

main web page for a business, organization or person

a handheld computer that serves as a personal organizer

d. coding language used to create documents on the Internet

e. a measurement of how fast data is moved from one place to another

The answers are:

a. -10 – (-5) = -10 + 5 = -5

b. 12 – (8) = 12 + -8 = 4

c. -15 – (-23) = -15 + 23 = 8

d. 9 – (-18) = 9 + 18 = 27

e. 0 – (18) = 0 + -18 = -18

f. $^1/_2$ – ($-^3/_4$) = $^1/_2$ + $^3/_4$ = $^5/_4$ or $1^1/_4$

Solution #96

The answers are:

c. PDA

b. home page

e. bps

d. HTML

a. password

Percents to Decimals

Workout #97

ne word *percent* means "parts of a hundred." To convert a percent to a decimal, you divide by)0. The easiest method of converting is to move the decimal point two places to the left (the ıme as dividing by 100).

irections: Convert the following percents to decimals:

9% = _____   d. 600% = _____   g. $3\frac{1}{3}$% = _____

67% = _____   e. .5% = _____

0.2% = _____   f. 9.45% = _____

Here's a Tip!

Workout #98

hen dining at a restaurant, you should leave a tip for your server that is 15% of the total price of meal.

termine the appropriate tips for the following bills:

a. $8 _____

b. $25.40 _____

c. $63.70 _____

The answers are:

a. 9% = .09

b. 67% = .67

c. 0.2% = .002

d. 600% = 6

e. .5% = .005

f. 9.45% = .0945

g. $3\frac{1}{3}$ % = .0333

Solution #98

To find 15% of a number, multiply it by 0.15.

Here's how:

a. $8 = 8 x .15 = $1.20

b. $25.40 = 25.40 x .15 = 3.81

c. $63.70 = 63.70 x .15 = 9.555 ≈ $9.56

Carmen's Monthly Allowance

e following is a circle graph displaying Carmen's
onthly allowance. Review the budget then answer the
estions below.

What percentage does Carmen spend for school lunch-
es and clothes? _____

How much more does Carmen spend on savings than
on miscellaneous items? _____

f Carmen's monthly budget is $75, how much does
he spend on movies? _____

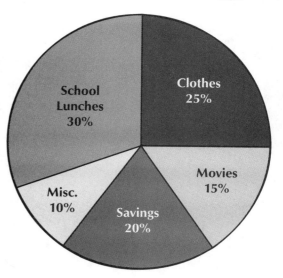

B	I	N	G	O
-2	-4	-3	-1	8
$5^1/_2$	3	-7	9	-5
0	7	FREE	-9	5
1	-6	4	10	-11
2	6	-8	$2^1/_4$	-10

ections: Cross out the correct answers to the following problems:

5 – (-3) = _____   d. -2 ÷ ($-^1/_4$) = _____

3 – 5 = _____   e. -3 + 4 ÷ -1 = _____

5)($-^1/_2$) = _____   f. -4 × (2 – 3) = _____

The answers are:

a. 30% + 25% = 55%

b. 20% – 10% = 10%

c. $75 x .15 = $11.25

The answers are:

B	I	N	G	O
~~-2~~	-4	~~-3~~	-1	~~8~~
$6^{1}/_{2}$	3	~~-7~~	9	-5
0	7	~~FREE~~	-9	5
1	-6	~~4~~	10	-11
2	6	~~-8~~	$2^{1}/_{4}$	-10

a. -5 – (-3) = -2
b. -3 – 5 = -8
c. (6)(-$^{1}/_{2}$) = -3
d. -2 ÷ (-$^{1}/_{4}$) = 8
e. -3 + 4 ÷ -1 = -7
f. -4 x (2 – 3) = 4

Teaching Tips

#1

sson Planning

veloping lesson plans involves three lev-
of planning:
ong-term lesson planning
grading period (quarterly or semester)
planning
daily lesson planning

g-Term Lesson Planning

r curriculum guides, achievement stan-
ds, course objectives and math depart-
nt chairperson are the primary
urces for developing a long-term les-
plan. The entire school year should be
pped out in terms of units for each grad-
period. Long-term lesson plans should
ompass all curricula requirements and
uld be developed cognizant of all state-
e and district assessments. Adjustments
ong-term lesson plans should be made
he end of grading periods, based on
uctional achievements and additional
ds of your students.

ding Period Planning

ding period planning should be docu-
ted in a daily planner with specific
ctives for the lesson. Plans should be
ewed and revised on a weekly basis,
d on instructional achievements and
needs of students.

y Lesson Plans

daily lesson plan is a detailed blueprint
cribing the essential elements and
ities for the lesson. These plans should
eviewed and revised daily, based on
uctional achievements and the needs
udents. Daily lesson plans should be
eloped on individual sheets of
r/forms and filed for future use. There
also useful computer programs for
loping lesson plans. Lesson Plans for
dows® is one of the most recommended.

Effective daily plans contain the following
elements in some form or another:

1. **Workout:** Workouts are excellent tools for getting the math lesson started. Workouts can be used to introduce a lesson or as a tool to engage students with various mathematical concepts.
2. **Objective:** The lesson's objective is a specific description of the knowledge or skill that students should learn from the lesson.
3. **Introduction:** The introduction can include several elements:
   a. introducing the concept
   b. review of prerequisite skills
   c. an overview or demonstration of the skill
   d. a discussion of needed supplies and materials
   e. an exercise to grab students' interest and enthusiasm
4. **Instruction:** This is the core of the lesson. Methods of instruction will vary, depending of the topic, student learning styles, teaching styles/methods, student skill level and needs of the students.
5. **Independent and/or Group Practice:** Give students an opportunity to try the skill individually or as part of a group activity. Follow this practice with immediate feedback. Additional instruction/ demonstration and independent practice may be needed.
6. **Assessment of Lesson's Effectiveness:** Determine the effectiveness of the lesson and any remaining students' needs. Adjust your daily lesson plan if necessary. There are a number of ways to assess lesson effectiveness, including observing student work, asking questions, having students work problems at the chalkboard, short quizzes, etc.
7. **Summary/Review and Additional Practice (Homework):** At the end of the lesson, the teacher should provide a brief summary of the lesson. The lesson's objective should be reinforced through additional practice (homework, projects, special assignments).

Emergency Lesson Plans

Every teacher should maintain three sets of emergency lessons on file. These plans should be generic math lessons so they can be used anytime throughout the year. Helpful Tip: Videotape the lessons in advance. It's the next best thing to you being there!

Tip #2
Early Classroom Structure

An outstanding middle-school math teacher once said that the key to his success was not to smile for the first three months of the school year. Though the statement is not meant to be taken literally, the point, however, was well taken. In establishing classroom rules and expectations, it is best to start out the year with too much structure. It is far easier to ease restrictions as the school year progresses than to remedy problems caused by a weak classroom structure. Here are some suggestions for structuring your classroom.

1. Carefully plan and implement strategies that involve high expectations.
2. Establish classroom rules that are fair while promoting a classroom environment that is safe, orderly and conducive to learning.
3. Reinforce classroom rules and expectations. Display them clearly in your classroom.
4. Use assigned seating charts, desk labels and information cards to rapidly learn students' names, personalities and parent contact information.
5. Establish a protocol for everything: entering the classroom, exiting the classroom, asking questions, getting out of seats, turning in assignments, going to the restroom, talking in class, obtaining permission, bringing books and materials, etc.
6. Clearly define and enforce consequences for misbehavior.
7. Involve parents early and let them know your rules and expectations.
8. Don't make exceptions. It sends a message of vulnerability and indecisiveness.

Establishing structure early on in the school year will make the rest of the school year more manageable and enjoyable for you and your students.

Teaching Tips

Tip #3
Effective Classroom Management

It has been estimated that the average teacher in an urban setting spends at least one-third of classroom time on classroom-management related issues. This takes valuable time away from actual classroom instruction and is the number one factor that drives many teachers out of the profession. Here are some basic ABCs of classroom management to keep in mind:

A. **Atmosphere.** Effective classroom management involves creating an inviting atmosphere for learning, which includes a well-arranged and visually stimulating classroom, clear rules and expectations, enforced rules with definite consequences and instruction that is stimulating, exciting and applicable.

B. **Be prepared.** Preparation is key to effective classroom management. The better prepared you are, the more confident, relaxed and in control you are. Preparation not only involves developing outstanding lesson plans, it also means having a plan for dealing with distractions and disruptive students.

C. **Cooperation.** Remember that educating children is a collaborative effort, involving an entire "village" of people, like parents, administrators, counselors, peers, mentors, role models, community leaders, coaches and social workers. Helping students reach their full potential is a team endeavor. Know all the resources available to you and use them as much as possible.

Tip #4
Establishing Classroom Rules

The importance of establishing classroom rules is well-known. There are as many approaches to developing and implementing rules as there are rules themselves. Some teachers favor the idea of giving students a voice in establishing classroom rules others prefer to establish the rules themselves. No matter which approach you use, there are some key points you should keep in mind.

1. Classroom rules must be established from the first day of school and reinforced as frequently as possible.
2. Rules without consequences are not rules at all.

3. Classroom rules should be relevant, clear and concise and should be displayed and visible to all students in the classroom.
4. Students and parents should acknowledge their understanding of the classroom rules and the consequences for not following them. You could have students and parents sign a form describing the rules and consequences and keep the signed document on file.

Classroom rules should address the following issues:
1. Respectfulness for all people and property
2. Classroom protocol
3. Expectations regarding preparedness, attendance, promptness, attentiveness, assignment completion, effort and honesty
4. Classroom disruptions and consequences for rule violations

Example of Rules Acknowledgement Form

Classroom Rules
Mrs. Smith-Jones Math Class

1. Students will be respectful and courteous to all people.
2. Students will be in their assigned seats, prepared for class and ready to work when the bell rings.
3. Students will obtain permission before speaking or leaving their desks.
4. Students will pay attention and always try their hardest.
5. Students will respect school property and the property of others.
6. Classroom disruptions, cheating and dishonesty will not be tolerated.
7. Assignments should be completed and turned in on time. Late and incomplete work is subject to penalty.
8. Students will obey classroom rules at all times. Consequences for not following rules include: loss of privileges, parent conferences, detention and administrative action (suspension, expulsion).

I fully understand the classroom rules presented above, and I intend to follow these rules to the best of my ability.

_____ _____ _____ _____
Student   Date   Parent   Date

Tip #5
Fostering Parental Involvement

Effective and consistent school-home communication is a critical component of dent success and achievement. Reseashows that parental involvement has a itive affect on students' attitudes towschool and particular subject arParental involvement improves studeclassroom behavior, time spent on howork, expectation for the future, abteeism, motivation and retention.school district and school may alrehave strategies in place to promparental involvement. However, here afew tips that you can use at the classrolevel to foster greater parental invoment:

1. Utilize current technology. If school or district has a Web site, usIf not, work with others in your scand community to develop one. (Tare also Web sites available k12.finalsite.com and www.teacher.com.) Use e-mail or the site to communicate regularly withparents and students. Parents canly communicate with teachers via eand receive automatic e-mail notition of unexcused absences, misassignments, failing grades, behavconcerns, upcoming assignmentsexams.

2. Make telephone calls to the paperiodically. Know their work phnumbers, home phone numbers, phone numbers, physical addressese-mail addresses. Phone calls that vide updates on student successesthe areas where they need impment will be appreciated by paren

3. Have parents sign and return as tests, quizzes and assignments as ble. Periodically send home indiviized notes, greetings and notices toents.

Teaching Tips

Make your classroom inviting and celebrate parent participation. Encourage parents to participate by having special lessons, field trips, presentations and activities that include them.

Schedule periodic parent/teacher conferences at school. Look at these conferences as an opportunity for you and the parents to work as a team to help the student.

...e parents aware of how their involve...t can benefit their children. Parent ...lvement is the most valuable resource ...elping students succeed in their future ...ers.

#6
Skill Building,
Short Frequent Quizzes

...of the best ways to improve students' ...computational skills is to give short, ...uent quizzes. These quizzes should ...e from three to eight problems and ...ld be able to be completed in a short ...unt of time. Give feedback and ...w the solutions as soon as possible— ...ter than the next class meeting.

...tron grading machines using multiple-...ce scantron grade sheets make these ...zes easy for teachers. Scantron grad-...nachines can be set to provide instant ...back on the areas of students' ...gths and weaknesses. If your math ...rtment or school does no use this ...oment, work with other teachers, ...nistrators and parents to obtain it. If ...do not have the equipment, you can ...have fellow students grade papers or ...student grade their own.

...t student progress on the quizzes. ...quiz grades should be weighed at a ...that does not elicit text/quiz anxiety, ...nake the quizzes significant enough ...at students will be encouraged to do ...best. Quizzes should include cumu-...items from previous units, areas that ...improvement and skills from current ...You will be amazed by the effective-...of this technique in building and main-...g student skill levels and in building ...nt confidence.

Tip #7
Multiplication Tables: The Root of Many Problems

Middle school math teachers will tell you that multiplication tables mastery is important for their students' success in mathematics. Students who do not master this skill, at least for numbers 1-12, are severely limited in their ability to progress in mathematics. Without knowledge of multiplication facts, students have more difficulty mastering division, fractions, percents, decimals and algebraic concepts. Memorization is the most effective method of achieving multiplication knowledge. By memorizing, students develop a solid knowledge base, skill development, conceptual understanding, application and mastery.

Be sure to test your students' multiplication table skills early on. Test knowledge and speed. If students are lacking speed or accuracy, provide additional resources to get them up to standard. These resources could include tutoring, flash cards, drills or parent involvement with a plan for additional practice at home.

As you drill your students, use timed exercises that combine several operations to further enhance students' knowledge, speed and confidence. For example,

1. $8 \times 11 =$
2. $72 \div 12 =$
3. $2 \times 9 \div 3 =$
4. $6 \times (11 - 4) =$
5. $3^3 =$
6. $6 \times 7 =$
7. $48 \div 4 =$
8. $14 - 2 \times 6 =$
9. $(9 \times 2) + (11 \times 12) =$
10. $7^2 - 11 =$

The time and attention spent on multiplication table mastery will pay big dividends throughout the course of the school year.

Tip #8
Teaching Students with Special Needs

All students are unique, with unique personalities and characteristics. However, there are certain students with special challenges that have to be addressed in order for them to have the same opportunities to succeed in school. These students are our special education students. By the reauthorization of the Individuals with Disabilities Act (IDEA) in 2004, all special education students should have an Individualized Education Program (IEP) designed to meet their unique needs.

As a regular classroom teacher, you are required by law to implement the IEPs of your special education students. The following tips will help you:
1. Know which students have IEPs.
2. Read each IEP thoroughly.
3. Insert in a summary of each student's modifications and accommodations in your planning book.
4. When recommended by the IEP team, allow students to use assistive technology (calculators, computers, etc.).
5. Participate in IEP meetings at every opportunity.
6. Incorporate the needs of special needs students in your lesson plans.
7. Work closely with your special education teacher(s) and involve the parents.

ED Students. More likely than not, at least one or more of your students have a disability that falls in the category of emotional disturbance (ED). For more information, contact Office of Special Education (OSEP) at *OSEP@ed.gov*. There is a movement among educational professions to emphasize the term "behaviorally disordered," which is believed to be a less stigmatizing label than "emotional disturbance" found in IDEA.

These students exhibit a broad range of behaviors that may impede their educational performance (and the performance of other students). There is a great deal of research and instructional strategies on teaching ED students available, including Positive Behavioral Supports (PBS), methods of modifying teaching styles and expectations and ways to tolerate negative behaviors. Here are some practical tips to help you meet this growing challenge in public education:
1. Involve the parents, administrators, counselors and other support staff (special education resource teachers, school psychologist, school social worker as much as possible. Participate in student IEP meetings. Articulate your concerns and develop strategies and support that will best serve the students.

Teaching Tips

2. Insist that ED students abide by the same classroom rules as other students. Do not allow them to take control of your classroom. If other students observe disruptive behavior, it will undermine your authority as a teacher and your ability to maintain a safe and orderly learning environment.

3. For students who are not responsive or are persistently disruptive, request a special education resource teacher be with you in the classroom. The student is required to have one if recommended by the IEP team. The special education resource teacher can remove the student temporarily to alternate setting when he or she is too disruptive.

4. Incorporate proven strategies:
   a. behavior contracts
   b. positive reinforcements
   c. time-outs
   d. traditional consequences for misbehavior

5. Maintain your self-control at all times. Don't belittle or embarrass the students. Don't get in a power struggle with them, but don't let them get away with being disobedient.

Tip #9
Teaching At-Risk Students

At-risk students are at a greater risk of failure and/or dropping out of school than other students. Socio-economic factors often have the greatest impact in this determination. Many of these students come from poor neighborhoods and have minimal parental support and involvement in their education. Arguably, teaching at-risk students is the most demanding and challenging assignment in the teaching profession. If you have at-risk students, here are some practical tips to help you:

1. Create a classroom culture that promotes success. Map out a course for students to achieve success and show them how to navigate it. At-risk students need to believe that
   a. success is attainable
   b. they control their own success and future

   c. their efforts and commitment will be rewarded
   d. you believe that they will succeed

The best way to establish a classroom culture/climate that is nurturing and supportive is by positively addressing your students. As a teacher, you have to sell them on themselves and your belief that success is attainable for each of them. Reinforce this at every opportunity.

2. Remain supportive and maintain discipline. Sometimes being supportive and nurturing has become synonymous with being lax and weak. When dealing with at-risk students, you need to implement even greater structure, rely more on your classroom management skills and apply greater discipline with firm consequences for misbehavior. However, you must emphasize to your students that your demands and expectations are part of the formula for their success.

3. Turn basic skill development into activities that are meaningful and engaging. Too often, at-risk students are tracked into substandard courses with low expectations. Though such courses provide an adequate review of basic math skills, the courses do little to inspire students. Current research suggests at-risk students should be involved in learning that is meaningful and engaging. As a teacher of at-risk students, you must be creative in your efforts. Discover and implement ways of incorporating basic math skills into activities that are practical, meaningful and engaging.

4. Involve the parents. Don't assume that parents of at-risk students don't want to be involved. Most parents do want to be involved in the child's education. They are looking for ways to be involved. Be persistent in seeking parental involvement. If your first few efforts are unsuccessful, keep trying. Your very next effort could be the one that makes the difference.

5. Implement a tutoring program. If at all possible, implement a tutoring program, before or after school for one hour each week. Often, at-risk students will respond better in small groups or in one-on-one settings. A tutoring program is an excellent way to provide students with extra help, to mentor and counsel students and foster healthy student-teacher relationships.

6. Rely on available support. Use supp[...] personnel and support systems a[...] able to you. Involve school adminis[...]tors, program coordinators, counsel[...] mentors, parole officers, parents [...] other support staff. Finally, organ[...]tions like Big Brother/Big Sister, [...] Black Men and other volunteer org[...]zations within your educational c[...]munity can be useful.

Tip #10
Become Your Own Resour[...]

A major key to becoming a succe[...] teacher is to stockpile an arsenal of r[...]ence materials, lessons plans, assessn[...] instruments (test and quizzes) and n[...] detailing proven approaches/strategie[...] other words, become your own resou[...] The following are ways that you can [...]cessfully accomplish this:

1. Organize and maintain files. Inc[...] lesson plans that you have develo[...] and ones that you discovered that [...] successful and appealing. You sh[...] keep at least one copy of all the [...] and quizzes on file. Include curricu[...] guides, articles, tips and notes [...] your teaching experiences. Also n[...]tain a file of the telephone numbers [...] addresses of people and organiza[...] that can be helpful to you as a tea[...]

2. Maintain a personal library of [...] books, reference books, educati[...] videos and DVDs. From time to [...] videotape your own lessons and [...] them in your personal library.

3. Develop and store your own [...] warm-ups. When you think of an i[...] esting problem or see an intrig[...] idea, write it down and save it.

4. Bookmark useful Web sites.

5. Do your own research and keep [...] on effective teaching methods [...] strategies.

6. Do your reading. On the nights [...] always have one fun book and [...] book related to the profession of t[...]ing.